Dramatically Good Geography

Geographical
Association

Photo: Brin Best

Theory INTO Practice

PROFESSIONAL DEVELOPMENT
FOR GEOGRAPHY TEACHERS
Series editors: Mary Biddulph and Graham Butt

Dramatically Good Geography

**MARY BIDDULPH
AND
GAYNOR BRIGHT**

Geographical
Association

Acknowledgements

The authors would like to thank Dr Margaret Sands for her constructive and supportive feedback during the writing of this book.

The Geographical Association would like to thank Brin Best, Peter Fox, John Harrison, Margaret Roberts and Diane Swift for permission to use the photographs that appear in this book.

The authors

Mary Biddulph is Lecturer in Geography Education in the School of Education, University of Nottingham, and Gaynor Bright is Head of Performing Arts at The Long Eaton School, Derbyshire.

The series editors

Mary Biddulph is Lecturer in Geography Education in the School of Education, University of Nottingham, and Dr Graham Butt is Senior Lecturer in Geographical Education in the School of Education, University of Birmingham.

ISBN 1 84377 053 9
First published 2003
Impression number 10 9 8 7 6 5 4 3 2 1
Year 2007 2006 2005 2004
Published by the Geographical Association, 160 Solly Street, Sheffield S1 4BF. The Geographical Association is a registered charity: no 313129.

The Publications Officer of the GA would be happy to hear from other potential authors who have ideas for geography books. You may contact the Officer via the GA at the address above. The views expressed in this publication are those of the author and do not necessarily represent those of the Geographical Association.

Copy edited by Rose Pipes
Designed by Bryan Ledgard
Printed by Espace Grafic, Spain

Contents

Editors' preface

Theory into Practice is dedicated to improving both teaching and learning in geography. The over-riding element in the series is direct communication with the classroom practitioner about current research in geographical education and how this relates to classroom practice. Geography teachers from across the professional spectrum will be able to access research findings on particular issues which they can then relate to their own particular context.

How to use this series

This series also has a number of other concerns. First, we seek to achieve the further professional development of geography teachers and their departments. Second, each book is intended to support teachers' thinking about key aspects of teaching and learning in geography and encourages them to reconsider these in the light of research findings. Third, we hope to reinvigorate the debate about how to teach geography and to give teachers the support and encouragement to revisit essential questions, such as:

- Why am I teaching this topic?
- Why am I teaching it in this way?
- Is there a more enjoyable/challenging/interesting/successful way to teach this?
- What are the students learning?
- How are they learning?
- Why are they learning?

This list is by no means exhaustive and there are many other key questions which geography teachers can and should ask. However, the ideas discussed and issues raised in this series provide a framework for thinking about practice. Fourth, each book should offer teachers of geography a vehicle within which they can improve the quality of teaching and learning in their subject; and an opportunity to arm themselves with the new understandings about geography and geographical education. With this information teachers can challenge current assumptions about the nature of the subject in schools. The intended outcome is to support geography teachers in becoming part of the teaching and learning debate. Finally, the series aims to make classroom practitioners feel better informed about their own practice through consideration of, and reflection upon, the research into what they do best – teach geography.

Mary Biddulph and Graham Butt
September 2003

Introduction

Could a classroom be a rainforest, a waste site, the top of a mountain, a national park and 25 individuals with their own experiences, perspectives, values and beliefs?

The aim of this book is to consider what opportunities exist for using drama strategies in geography classrooms and how such imagined experiences can contribute to key stage 3 students' geographical learning. We explore such questions as:

- How can students be given opportunities thoroughly to explore their own values, beliefs and opinions through geography?
- How can geography help students begin to understand the values and beliefs of others?
- How can geography contribute to students' understanding of complex people-environment relationships in a way that will enable them to develop informed arguments, reassess their values, and critically evaluate their perspectives and those of others?

The literature which explores effective communication in the geography classroom is wide-ranging and includes material on classroom talk (Roberts, 1986; Leat, 2000, Butt, 2001) as well as the use of simulations (Walford, 1996; Joyce et al., 2000). However, little has been written on the use of drama methods to enhance geographical learning. While the QCA Schemes of Work (2000) advocate the use of drama in aspects of teaching and learning, for example Unit 3: People everywhere, Unit 6: World Sport, and Unit 18: The global fashion industry, what is needed is an exploration of the 'Why?' and 'How?' of the use of drama in the geography classroom.

This book draws the experiences of key stage 3 students and Post-graduate Certificate in Education (PGCE) students using drama to contribute to learning in geography. Chapters 1 and 2 discuss the nature of creative talking and how it can become part of the geography curriculum. Chapters 3 and 4 explore the practical issues surrounding the use of drama in the classroom and offer suggestions for ways of implementing drama strategies. Chapters 5 and 6 consider the implications of the use of drama for teachers and students, and Chapter 7 considers how to assess geographical understanding as a consequence of drama activities in geography.

It is not our intention to convert geography teachers into drama teachers, but rather to consider the unique contribution drama methods can make to the understanding of geographical concepts.

Photo: Margaret Roberts

1: Creative talk in geography

Creativity and being creative is nothing new to geography teachers, it is what they do best. They creatively interpret subject content, ideas, events and experiences so that students of all ages, abilities and interests can learn. Being an effective geography teacher *requires* creativity.

What does creativity in the geography curriculum actually look like? Rawling and Westaway (2003) extract three overlapping themes from the CAPE-UK Project (NFER, 1998) - Expressive, Imaginative and Critical thinking. They identify them as the means through which geography can contribute to creativity, and vice versa (Rawling and Westaway, 2003, p. 5). Durbin offers a slightly different model: the Creativity wheel. Here the role of the teacher is that of a facilitator who advises, encourages and assures, thus ensuring that students are enabled to use their imagination, be original, pursue purpose and make judgements about values (Durbin, 2003, p. 65). Both models advocate that the content-driven geography curriculum can now be put to one side in favour of a curriculum that enables students to explore geographical concepts in a more critical and thoughtful way.

Talking in geography

Communication takes many different forms in busy classrooms - writing, listening, body language, observing and *talking* – but student talk is frequently banished to the margins of learning activities. Classroom talk tends to be dominated by the teacher (Butt, 2000). Yet talking is how most young people communicate most of the time. They talk when considering an idea or an issue, when they explain thoughts and feelings, and when they express concerns and opinions, as well as at other times. Young people in and out of school have a natural tendency to talk: in friendship groups, on the telephone, with their family,and during play. They use talk in a wide variety of social settings and for a range of purposes.

Where students are given the opportunity to talk in the classroom, the talk is often limited and highly controlled. For example, they may answer a series of closed questions, or discuss a particular idea where specific outcomes are required. Such forms of classroom talk can limit the learning process in geography as the opportunity to explore new ideas is curtailed. Wider social and personal benefits to students are also lost as the opportunity to develop oral skills and self-confidence through purposeful talk is forfeited. Placing limits on talk, while seeming to be an effective form of managing behaviour can often be experienced by students as repressive and de-motivating.

The geography national curriculum is explicit in the expectation that geography should enable students to: 'communicate in ways appropriate to the task and audience' (DfEE/QCA, 1999a, p. 22), but it is only in the non-statutory element relating to key stage 1 that is it referred to directed. The non-statutory guidance for key stage 2 and key stage 3 refers only to 'building on' various aspects of the English curriculum, including 'En1: Speaking and listening' (DfEE/QCA, 1999b, p. 31).

The *Literacy Across the Curriculum* training materials (DfEE/SEU, 2001), for the Key Stage 3 Strategy, provide teachers with ideas and structures for organising group talk in the classroom, but the embedded message about 'talking' is very much to do with students talking, as themselves, in groups. Useful suggestions are made about different types of group structure, the pros and cons of different forms of group organisation, the problems associated with group work and what group talk can do for students. The practice advocated can apply to many different contexts and the explicit advice under the heading 'Golden rules' is that talk can and should be part of classroom events.

What is missing is any direct reference to drama as a means for encouraging exploratory and creative talk. At no point are teachers or students actively invited to step beyond the confines of the classroom into the world of the imagination, to use talk creatively in order to extend understanding.

How can creative talk be part of learning geography?

Leat notes that 'understanding develops through talk as ideas and interpretations are communicated and shared' (1998, p. 160). Based on the work of the National Oracy Project, he goes on to identify the indicators of quality talk in the classroom as being:

- **reciprocity**: where students, through talking in groups, appreciate the strengths and weaknesses of different ideas and thus work towards alternative solutions
- **speculation, making connections and interpreting**: where students start to pose themselves questions and 'ponder' alternatives
- **talking at length**: where students are able to explore their own thinking, justify their own ideas and offer their opinions in more than a few words and not necessarily in response to a teacher-directed question
- **students initiating**: where students, rather than the teacher, initiate discussion on a particular theme, topic or aspect of geography, and the teacher responds
- **teacher questions**: where the teacher dedicates more time to the use of open questions which enable students to speculate, interpret and reflect (Leat, 1998, p. 160).

What Leat is describing is the oral version of extended writing - extended talking. Extended talking affords students the opportunity to talk at length, talk in depth, use a wide range of vocabulary, explore their own ideas and those of others, express opinions, develop arguments and reveal feelings. Extended writing becomes creative writing when students are expected to use imaginative vocabulary and varied linguistic techniques, to explore and exploit language and to 'organise and structure material to convey ideas themes and characters' (DfEE, 2001, p. 37).

Photo: Diane Swift

A helpful way to think about the use of creative talk is in terms of styles of teaching. These styles can be grouped into three categories – closed, framed and negotiated – which describe the relative levels of student and teacher participation in the learning process, known as 'the participant dimension' (Figure 1, overleaf) (Roberts, 1996). The model, summarised in Figure 1, has been adapted to focus on creative talk. All three categories have their merits, depending on the context, content and degree of use in the classroom. However, in relation to developing students' creative talking skills, we are most interested in the 'negotiated' category.

Figure 1:
The participant dimension and classroom talk. After: Barnes et al., 1987.

	Style of teaching and learning		
	Closed	**Framed**	**Negotiated**
Content	Teacher led, subject content specific and not negotiable.	Teacher led but based upon an appreciation of students' perspectives.	Teachers and students contribute to shaping the content. Content becomes negotiable.
Focus	Teacher is subject expert; students have little to contribute.	Teacher is subject expert; students contribute their limited perspectives.	Teacher is facilitator; supports and prompts open-ended talk via key questions, probing and listening. Creative talk encouraged via use of resources, group processes and drama strategies.
Students' role	Listening. Any student talk is in response to teacher-led closed questions and is therefore limited in scope.	Contributors to more open-ended discussions.	Have responsibility to contribute and participate. Emphasis on listening and talking together creatively.
Key concepts	Teacher communicates knowledge to students.	Teacher shares knowledge with students and builds on their current level of understanding.	Students explore their current level of understanding and, through talking and sharing, deepen understanding of key geographical issues.
Methods	Subject-led exposition by teacher. Use of subject-specific language.	Exposition with discussions. Students given opportunities to contribute ideas, perspectives and opinions.	Group and whole-class talk. Students interrogate and critically evaluate geographical concepts using creative talk. They are responsible for their learning.

It is in the 'negotiated' category that students are encouraged to build on what they know, take a high degree of responsibility for the learning process, and shape and inform the learning outcomes. They are required to explore their own use of language and to use and apply different languages in different contexts. By this we do not necessarily mean modern foreign languages, although this is possible (see Coyle, 1996), but rather the language of others, which identify someone as an individual with particular perspectives, values and beliefs. It gives an opportunity to imagine what it might be like to 'be' someone else, to see the world through someone else's eyes.

Drama, as a vehicle for developing creative talk, enables students to use their imagination, prior knowledge and interests, as well as language, to investigate, enquire into, hypothesise about and explore new geographical ideas. It can lead to their assessment and re-assessment of perspectives (their own and others') while also developing a greater confidence, a sense of responsibility and enhanced self-esteem.

In this book, what is being proposed is that drama can be used as a vehicle for enabling key stage 3 students to develop their creative talking skills.

Photo: Peter Fox (Please note the quality of this image is low because it is taken from digital video source)

2: Defining drama

Nicholson (2000) identifies drama as being:

> 'both a discipline and ... a journey; it involves a synthesis of student-centred and subject-centred educational approaches. At its richest the drama curriculum embraces a range of cultural forms, includes a variety of aesthetic and artistic practices and introduces students to new ways of thinking and feeling. It is an uncertain, creative and sometimes haphazard process' (2000, p. 2).

Neelands (1992) offers a way of classifying the different contributions of drama to learning. These are shown in Figure 2 overleaf.

Drama in the geography classroom provides teachers with the much-needed opportunity to engage with the student-subject synthesis mentioned above. Drama in geography could involve techniques ranging from the simple, e.g. 'values continuum' (see page 19), to the more complex, e.g. role play, where students express the views and take on the values of someone else. As well as these two there are many drama techniques, which can be used as part of a geography teacher's repertoire of strategies. They are outlined in Chapter 4.

Why drama?

The geography national curriculum states that students at key stage 3 should be taught to:

> 'appreciate how people's values and attitudes, including their own, affect contemporary social, environmental, economic and political issues, and to clarify and develop their own values and attitudes about such issues' (DfEE/QCA, 1999a, p. 22).

Figure 2:
Aspects of drama.
Adapted from:
Neelands, 1992.

Context	Activity
A practical activity	Students make use of speech, space and movement in order to make meaning.
A form of shared cultural identity	Students have the opportunity to share and explore their own cultural identity as well as gain insights into the cultural ways and identities of other social groups.
A vehicle for exploring human nature and experience	Students can explore and express their own experiences and develop their understanding of central societal concepts through the use of concrete examples.
The taking on of roles and adopting different viewpoints in 'real' experiences	Students can view their own and other people's behaviour from unfamiliar perspectives. The emotional experience is real for the students even though the activity may have fictional elements. Students can participate in authentic experiences which may be very different from their own.
Generating vocal and active responses to fictional situations - a unique form of literacy	Students are asked to behave realistically in 'fictional' situations. They are expected to respond to, adapt and reshape ideas and understanding through language and action.
Developing the imagination's ability to 'make believe'	Students use their imagination to construct unfamiliar, but credible and coherent, contexts and situations.

Drama can be an invaluable tool in the delivery of this vital area of study because it:

- allows us to explore the complexities of people and issues (e.g. conflict situations);
- is oral, physical and visual, therefore accessible to students across the ability range;
- is a means of turning a mirror on the world to develop a better understanding of it;
- provides excellent opportunities to create evidence for Key Skills in Communication, Working with others, and Citizenship;
- aids the National Literacy drive, providing opportunities for the development of language and emotional literacy.

At the heart of all of this is the opportunity to use teaching strategies which combine the 'social, communicative, artistic, aesthetic, imaginative and rational' (NATE Drama Committee, 2000, p. 2). With drama, it is possible to move away from the two-dimensional (written work and pages in books), to the four-dimensional. Students can emerge from the relative safety of the space behind the desk and enter into a creative exploration with the teacher. The world of past, present and future is shaped and presented through moving images and words. Such techniques require a leap of faith and more imaginative approaches to assessment and to recording outcomes, but the potential for learning is tremendous.

The practicalities

Drama studios may seem full of noisy young people whose activity is unstructured and chaotic. But good drama activity balances periods of calm reflection and planning, with well-structured and highly participative experiences.

Dramatic activity will usually require a large free space. In an ordinary classroom this could be achieved by moving furniture. However it might be worth investigating the possibility of using a specialist space. Most drama teachers will be delighted to see geography teachers recognise the potential of drama, and be pleased to offer help and advice.

As well as seeking advice a good starting point could be to observe a drama lesson. During the observation, it is useful to consider key questions. These should include:

- How is the space organised?
- How are the students organised at different phases of the lesson?
- What specialist terms do the students and teacher use?
- How are students brought together for discussion, sharing work, re-focusing the task, and evaluation?
- How does the teacher stop activities to support, question and introduce new events and complications?

There are many educational drama handbooks on the market, which provide guidance both for specialists and non-specialists. We recommend Neelands and Goode (1990), O'Neill and Lambert (1982), Kempe and Ashwell (2000) and McGregor *et al.* (1987).

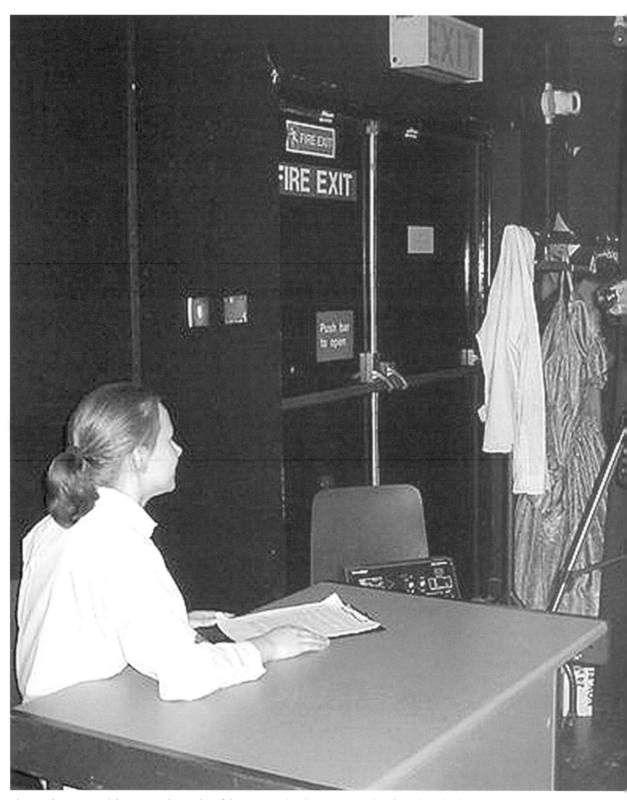

Photo: John Harrison (Please note the quality of this image is low because it is taken from digital video source)

3: Ideas for geography 3

The following drama methods and techniques are particularly well suited for use in geography lessons, and while these suggestions are open to interpretation, criticism and evaluation, they provide some ideas for getting started.

Values continuum

A useful technique for encouraging debate and for getting students to take a stand on an issue is to invite them physically to position themselves on a 'Values continuum'. A long, clear space in the room, such as a wide aisle between desks, is needed for this activity. Place two chairs at each end to represent opposite opinions. The teacher reads out a simple statement. If students are new to the technique, it can be helpful to start them off with a statement about something familiar to them, not necessarily geographical in nature. For example:
- I love football
- I am sensible with money

Students think about it, and decide whether they agree or disagree with the statement. Using a 'countdown to stillness' (raising both hands to indicate that the teacher needs stillness and quiet can be highly effective), students move to a position on the line that represents their opinion on the statement. Any shade of opinion between the extremes is possible, but students must be clear why they have chosen a particular position.

As students begin to understand the activity then issues of more geographical relevance can follow, such as:

- Everyone should have the right to roam in the countryside
- Sports and tourism should be restricted in National Parks
- There are too many restrictions on the development of land in rural areas

The whole class physically represents the range of options on the Values continuum and anyone can be challenged or questioned by the teacher or their peers. The teacher opens the debate by questioning those who represent the extremes, or those who have chosen the middle way. An extension of the activity might involve students re-positioning themselves following discussion. Who has moved? Why? Which of the arguments they have heard has been the most persuasive? Students can record their experience in diagrammatic form and write about the reasons for their choice of position.

Still image

A still image may also be referred to as a freeze-frame, statue, tableau or photograph. Creating 'still images' is easy to manage and develop, and is an ideal technique when using drama activities for the first time in geography. It is a very useful tool for engaging students in empathetic responses to people and situations because it is highly structured and focused. It can be used as part of other drama conventions to ensure student engagement and commitment.

Using this technique, students could enact a 'photograph' to accompany a newspaper headline, such as 'Flood devastates local homes', or 'Foot and mouth – the farmers' story'. The image developed by the students could be recorded using a digital camera and inserted into a document produced using a computer.

Extend the activity by asking different groups of students to create still images that represent a range of opposing views or particular situations, for example:

Situation 1: Land-use conflict
- Ramblers who find a footpath closed.
- A farming family who have lost livestock due to stray dogs.
- A local council meeting being disrupted by angry members of protest groups.

Situation 2: Developing tourism in less economically developed countries
- A group of tourists arriving at an airport in Indonesia.
- Local construction workers on the site of a new luxury hotel in the Maldives.
- Farmers and indigenous people being forcibly removed from their lands in Brazil.
- Government officials agreeing a contract with a multi-national hotel chain in Jamaica.

These images might be developed in several ways (see below). It is vital to stipulate that everyone must participate in the image and they must have a specific role and opinion. Students must not 'opt out' and play a tree, a sheep or a signpost!

Teachers can question students as they develop the images, to help them to clarify their thinking and intentions in shaping the image. Questions such as 'Who are you?', ' What are you doing?', 'Why are you here?', and 'What is your purpose?', will establish students' general level of understanding. These questions can then lead on to more probing questions such as 'In what ways will this affect you?', 'What are the long-term consequences of this action?', 'What are the alternatives?', and 'What are the implications in the short and medium term of pursuing a different course of action?'. These questions are essential to unearthing students' understanding and require them to deconstruct their own images for a wider audience. The questions are vital in that they are the vehicle through which you can:

- check the response for small groups and the whole class;
- deepen students' responses;
- develop and extend the work into more complex areas of geography;
- re-define the context for the learning;
- build belief into the work;
- evaluate/assess understanding.

(Adapted from: Taylor, 1991.)

While conducting a sequence of questioning you can choose to be either in role, as part of the drama, or remain separate, as the geography teacher.

Thought-tracking

Thought-tracking is a technique that can be used to highlight character, place and situation in relation to a still image. The teacher can ensure that students have engaged by asking them to speak the thoughts of the character they are portraying. A useful analogy for students is the comic-strip convention of the thought bubble. Students can present their image to the class and deepen identification and empathy by speaking the thought-tracks of the characters in turn. The shaping of the image and choice of characters can be discussed, or presented in written or diagrammatic form.

Staging a public enquiry

There are numerous examples in the geography classroom of situations in which role play, thought-tracking and other drama techniques can be applied to aid understanding. For example, staging a 'public enquiry' about a land-use proposal. The combined experience of participation (in the process) and reflection (through questioning in or out of role) can begin to provide students 'with insights into vital areas of human relationships' (Neelands, 1992, p. 21).

Students work in realistic 'interest groups' to prepare their contributions to a public enquiry. The preparation for the enquiry should be done within a tight time frame. As students are unlikely to have any experience of real public enquiries, it is advisable to explore any necessary language plus the format, structures and procedures of such a meeting in advance. Students representing different interest groups are encouraged to speak their thoughts in role. The teacher can either step back from the event and allow the process to be run by the students or can thought-track or still-image selected aspects of it as a strategy to check understanding. The audience can also be involved by freeze-framing and thought-tracking their thoughts and ideas as the enquiry unfolds.

Using a video camera to film the proceedings will provide a permanent record of contributions which will help the teacher to mark the oral work and quality of the artefacts, maps, testimony, statistics, etc., that are presented in the debate. Teachers could use a rubric to assess various aspects of the activity (see Chapter 7)

Hot seating

Hot seating is a convention much used in drama, and by English teachers to explore characters in novels and short stories. It can be used to advantage in the geography classroom – though it takes some self-confidence on the part of the geography teacher.

Instead of using a textbook to present the flora, fauna and river systems of the Amazon Basin, the teacher becomes an explorer who has recently returned from a trip to the Amazon rainforest. Students have to write an article for the school magazine, based on an interview with the explorer. The teacher uses pictures, artefacts, costume, recorded birdsong, samples of river water and anything else that brings added reality to the situation.

For such a strategy the classroom needs to be reorganised and specific ground rules established. Students arrange themselves in a semicircle around a central chair. They have a unique opportunity to talk to someone who has really been to a rainforest, and must find out as much as possible about the climate, river system, animals and plants, as well as the lifestyles, challenges and threats to the indigenous population.

To set the scene it is advisable for the teacher to make a short introductory speech in-role as the explorer. An example might be:

'Good morning. Thank you very much for inviting me to come and talk to you. It's a long time since I was last here - the place hasn't changed much! I understand that you have plenty of questions for me about my latest expedition. I've brought along some items to show you and I'm looking forward to reading the finished article in the school magazine. So, who has the first question?'

Students should raise their hand if they have a question and the teacher can make eye contact and nod to indicate who may speak. They should attempt to jot down important details and information to form the basis of their news report or article.

Still in role the teacher can encourage questions from those who have not spoken. If the class finds it difficult to accept the fiction, the teacher can come out of role by leaving the chair to re-focus the task, returning to the chair when the class is ready. Support from an older student, either as facilitator or interviewee, may be helpful. If such an activity is to be convincing and if the Amazon is to come alive for the students, it is essential that the geography teacher has an excellent grasp of the subject content as well as the ability to interpret it in relation to the type of questions asked.

The Amazon scenario is only one of a number of potential uses for hot-seating. The class could interview a controversial figure, for example the head of the multi-national hotel chain who argues for the benefits of global tourism, or two individuals with contrasting opinions on a geographical issue could be in the 'hot seat'. A development of the method is to move students from a still image to be hot-seated and to provide them with the opportunity to express their views and dilemmas. And again, a video or audio recording will allow the teacher to evaluate the students' engagement with the geographical issue or theme being explored.

To enhance the sense of realism, and an engagement with their roles, students can be encouraged to write diaries, letters to newspapers, or other written reports. Writing as if from the experience of the character will help them to understand the real issues from the perspective of those most closely involved.

Documentary

Having completed an initial study of land-use conflict in, say, the Peak District National Park, the whole class could work collaboratively to create a documentary. This will clearly take time - ideally several lessons. A video camera can add a touch of realism, and the resulting film will support the assessment process.

As a first step, the class as a whole can discuss and record typical features of documentary programmes. Elements might include expert witnesses (hot-seating), studio discussions, narrative/voice-over, photographs (still images), maps, models, charts, diagrams, documents, interviews with representatives of various interest groups, letters to newspapers, sound effects, costumes ... the list is a long as time allows and as broad as the students' imaginations.

The class can then discuss and agree a structure for the documentary using scoreboards and writing frames where appropriate. Tasks for completing the documentary are then given to groups, pairs or individuals, differentiated by ability, with everyone working towards a common goal. Strict time limits should be set for classroom and homework preparation. Using a large 'pie-chart' clock on the board, blocking it out as time is used up, helps to increases pace and challenge.

The teacher can either take on the role of editor or delegate it to a team whose brief is to achieve balance, monitor progress and sequence the filming.

Assessment can be oral (audio or video taped), or of a personal written diary with reflections on the process and final product. Writing frames and storyboards can be used to support students with literacy problems. Students can be assessed through teacher observation and notes, audio/video tape evidence, peer assessment and self-evaluation. Key questions or a rubric (see Figure 6, page 40) can be used to guide the assessment.

As an alternative to a television documentary, the class could produce one for the radio. Both types of documentary require written scripts, although for the radio broadcast students will, of course, need to take account of the absence of visual images.

The development of a radio script will require them to consider the geographical content, the use of geographical terminology and the geographical concepts they are trying to express, as well as generic issues such as structure, audience and presentation (pace, voice tone and inflection). For some, a radio presentation can remove some of the presentational pressures that other drama methods may create. In either case the students are being given the opportunity to 'communicate in ways appropriate to the task and the audience' in engaging and creative ways.

Photo: Brin Best

4: A question of pedagogy

Teaching strategies

Balderstone asserts that:

> 'There is (also) something about successful teaching that is difficult to put your finger on. The interplay between effective teaching and successful learning has sometimes been described as artistry. The idea of artistry recognises that teaching is a highly creative and personal activity' (2000, p. 128).

If geography teachers are to use drama techniques and strategies in their teaching, it is necessary for them to draw on their creative skills and qualities *and* to create the physical and intellectual environment which enables learning to take place. What this means in practice, is that geography teachers are going to need to draw more fully on what Shulman refers to as: 'pedagogical content knowledge, that special amalgam of content and pedagogy that is uniquely the province of teachers, their own special form of professional understanding' (1999, p. 64). Drama strategies require students to step outside the traditional comfort zone of the geography classroom into a more active and questioning space. The same is also required of the teacher. The teacher must change from being the one who offers the stimulus and constraints, as well as being the arbiter of what is worth studying and how to perform, to the one who:

- offers a range of resources with dramatic potential;
- can move the exploration on by offering new alternatives or helping students to find and keep a focus;
- asks questions which will challenge students' perceptions and intentions;
- sometimes plays the central role within the developing drama in order to heighten the students' experience;
- gives students new situations to respond to in their playing of dramatic roles, and interacts with the class as a researcher.

The potential of this kind of pedagogy is that the students' as well as the teacher's voices are heard and *valued*. Students are genuine participants in their own learning.

We are not asking geography teachers to become actors. What is required of the teacher is that, when necessary, she or he also *participates* in the drama process. The teacher adopts a set of attitudes, and takes up a particular stance in relation to a particular issue, seriously and with commitment. This way teachers will model the approach they expect from the students; they demonstrate to the class the significance of the lesson, and they can also intervene in the geographical learning taking place without detracting from the drama process. There are times during drama-geography lessons when the teacher will need to adopt more than one role in a lesson, possibly moving in and out of role to support individuals and groups, to manage the pace of the lesson and to evaluate learning. Essentially, the teacher is integral to as well as instigator of the pedagogical process.

For this to happen the role of geography teachers must change. They must at all times remain focused on being geography teachers – individuals with the subject knowledge base and pedagogical understanding to shape and inform learning – they must also, at times, to be more than this. For some this may feel risky – but being creative is a risky business.

Lambert issues a word of warning when it comes to thinking about such an active pedagogy:

> 'the employment of specific teaching techniques does not, on its own, necessarily produce worthwhile educational experience in terms of taking students further in their moral growth. A particular technique may be engaging and enjoyable ... But no matter how attractive such activities may appear in themselves they must not be allowed to become the ends rather than the means ... We need to ask where the lesson has taken us' (1999, p. 14).

We do need to be able to answer the question 'where has the lesson has taken us?' if drama lessons are to have a purpose. But answering such a question is not straightforward, and we need to be open-minded about our response. Where a lesson is taking us may only be revealed as the drama unfolds, and what it has achieved may only become clear when members of the class reflect on their experiences. But what drama can achieve is the *involvement* of all students in ways that suit their differing abilities and aptitudes, thus helping to make geography lessons active, interesting and purposeful.

Planning for drama lessons

Interviews with PGCE geography student teachers about their experiences of using drama during their teaching practice indicate that the geography curriculum can be managed in such a way as to create the time and opportunity to use drama strategies as part of teaching and learning. During the PGCE course, all student teachers had participated (although not necessarily comfortably) in a workshop which focused on the use of a range of drama strategies to support learning in geography. The drama workshop was presented as an opportunity to expand their teaching repertoire and to consider how they could balance geographical learning with interesting practical experiences.

The ensuing discussions produced a planning framework for drama strategies. Joyce *et al.* (2000) suggest a nine-stage model for embedding role play within the curriculum (what they describe as a 'syntax'), while Roberts (2003) suggests a seven-stage model, also for role play. The framework shown in Figure 3 takes account of a broader range of drama strategies.

Figure 3: A five point planning framework for drama lessons in geography.

---

1. Initial teaching around a topic or theme
- Can last for several lessons and involves a range of learning activities.
- New terminology and key concepts are introduced and explained.

2. Setting up of the drama
- Geographical objectives identified, and an overview of the drama is established with students.
- Students work in small groups, as decided by the teacher.
- Students use stimulus resources such as stories, newspaper reports, maps, photographs.
- Students are usually provided with a structure to organise their thinking and time-frames are set.
- Assessment processes and criteria are identified.

3. Planning the drama
- Students are given a fairly free rein in relation to planning, and are expected to be reasonably self-managing.
- Students are encouraged to be inventive and to use props to help to make any drama feel more real.
- Teacher acts as a manager of the class and supports small groups, offering advice, clarification and encouragement.

4. Delivering the drama
- Groups or individuals present/perform their contribution to the rest of the class. This could take the form of role-play, freeze-frame or the 'mantle of the expert'.
- The rest of the class are frequently, in or out of a role, given the opportunity to ask questions, challenge assumptions and seek clarification on relevant points.
- Students are praised for their contribution.
- The teacher can take on a role, to help to manage the activity.

5. Post drama
- Preparing some key questions is essential to support the de-briefing process.
- This phase varies according to the aims of the lesson. Students may be asked to use their learning to produce a piece of extended writing, usually imaginative, to demonstrate what they have learned as a consequence of the drama process.

Sometimes the drama itself provides evidence for assessment. The teacher, and possibly the rest of the class, provides feedback.

Photo: Diane Swift

Layered on to this framework has to be a clear understanding of the needs and abilities of students and insights into the social networks that influence student-student relationships.

The PGCE students found that the preparation phase was essential in setting the context for any drama activity, and that drama could be used in a range of ways for the exploration of different geographical concepts. They used a wide range of visual

resources such as maps (e.g. Ordnance Survey, atlas, hypothetical locational), photographs (e.g. of the countryside, of coastal erosion) and television programmes (e.g. the weather forecast, *Emmerdale*, reports on the eruption of Mount St Helens), as well as some formal teaching to introduce new ideas and key geographical terminology. It was clear that students knew from the outset where the preparation phase was leading, i.e. towards a drama activity, and where they were going beyond the drama. In most cases the drama was not an end in itself but a means of exploring new ideas and concepts which was frequently followed by some form of writing activity.

There were variations in the way the student teachers conducted the setting up and planning phases. In one case, the decision to use drama (in the form of a weather forecast) was made spontaneously based on the interest of several groups of school students. In other cases, time was spent preparing students both in terms of their geographical knowledge and understanding and their expectations of the drama in which they were to participate. In all cases students worked in small groups, either selected by the teacher or in friendship groups. The groups enabled students to explore the geographical content of the lessons with each other and with the teacher. The role of the teacher was to support group discussions, to encourage students to contribute their ideas, and to challenge them to evaluate their ideas against those of others. Using probing questions and focusing students on the geographical issues under discussion helped to support groups who were struggling to get started. Many student teachers felt that as students' motivation was high at this point, low-key intervention was all that was needed to maintain the pace of discussions.

For lessons in which the drama was performed, advance preparation of the teaching room, time for students to prepare themselves, and being explicit about expectations were all common practice. To ensure maximum participation of the whole class, other pupils (the audience) were encouraged to acknowledge and be supportive of the performance of others, and to ask questions to sharpen their own thinking. In relation to questions asked, the pattern that seemed to emerge was that initial questions and their responses were somewhat shallow. However, as confidence grew and the process took hold students would begin to use their own geographical knowledge to ask more probing questions and to challenge opposing points of view.

Figure 4 overleaf provides a planning model in practice. It was used for a lesson where a student teacher embedded drama into a series of geography lessons on coastal management in Norfolk. The students were required to address two key questions:

1. What are the effects of the cliff collapse on people?
2. What might be done to slow down the rate of cliff collapse?

In another lesson, this time on land use conflict in a national park, photographic evidence, whole-class discussions and Ordnance Survey map work were the scene setters. Freeze-framing and thought-tracking were used to build on geographical knowledge and explore understanding. This way the teacher became involved in the drama process, ensuring that more probing questions were asked and different levels of understanding were demonstrated. Some students, as well as the teacher, were able to thought-track other students. The advantage of thought-tracking was that the teacher and the students could focus on both the geographical context of the lesson and also probe more deeply into how individuals and groups might feel about certain land use conflicts.

The planning process described above ensures that drama strategies are embedded in a broader framework of geographical learning. At its best, drama can afford students the opportunity to build on existing knowledge and also to set about the complex task of constructing new knowledge for themselves.

Figure 4: Putting the planning model into practice – a drama geography lesson on coastal management.

Stage	Activities
1. Initial teaching	• Area being studied introduced via Ordnance Survey map work. • Coastal erosion management strategies introduced via question and answer session, diagrams on a work sheet and an over-head transparency. • The idea of using drama in subsequent lessons was introduced at this stage.
2. Setting up	• Students in groups given a set of role cards outlining the different views of individuals: a house builder, tourist, hotel manager, professor of geography, coastal engineer, local resident. More difficult roles given to groups of higher achievers. • Groups become 'experts' in one particular role. Discussion of point of view of their role in comparison to others. Ideas recorded on paper. • Groups nominate one representative to communicate their views at a 'meeting'. • Students ask questions of each other to clarify meaning and challenge opinions. They start to explore the values and attitudes of other interest groups. • Teacher manages the learning via the role of a reporter – only those holding the microphone can talk. • Debriefing via open-ended questions teases out key arguments. • Role play for next lesson set as homework. Criteria introduced, timeframes set and expectations made clear.
3. Planning	• Students work in small groups planning their drama. They choose a genre in which to work. • Students draw on the ideas from the presentation to ensure that all views are evident in their drama. • Space is made available in school for groups to practice. • Students clear that they have to demonstrate new geographical understanding and an appreciation of conflict of opinions. • Students can bring in props to help them to get into role more easily.

4. Delivering	• Room prepared in advance to ensure space for the drama. • Students have 5-10 minutes to organise themselves. • Dramas presented to the rest of the class. Several different styles are adopted: courtroom drama, chat show, documentary, and a soap opera. • Students put a lot of effort into the presentations in terms of props, music, use of space, the writing of scripts. Students of all abilities participate and all have something to say. • Evidence within the dramas that students have gained new geographical knowledge and understanding, that they can apply this to construct an argument, that they appreciate the range of conflicts that can arise over an issue such as coastal management.
5. Post drama	• Students set about the task of producing a newspaper report on the conflict surrounding coastal management in Norfolk. They are given a loose framework within which to write, and distinct geographical questions that they have to answer. • Students draft and re-draft their written reports using a word processing package. • Very little teacher input is needed at this stage – students understand the main ideas and feel confident that they can draw on their geographical knowledge and understanding to write produce an imaginative piece of writing.

Photo: Margaret Roberts

5: A question of participation

Constructing learning

The psychologist Lev Vygotsky (1962) identified social interaction as crucial to the development of students' cognitive ability, and as the means by which they could begin to construct their own knowledge and understanding The process of talking in groups in relation to open-ended tasks provides opportunities for students to share perceptions, explore new ideas, and almost subconsciously review and re-establish their geographical understanding. The social interactions inherent in drama lessons mean that students can begin to construct, deconstruct and reconstruct common geographical assumptions in a creative way.

Participation

Lambert argues that it is 'morally careless' for teachers to teach complex geographical issues as if there were 'clearcut answers: "Preserving the rainforest is a good thing" or "the new local transport developments will reduce traffic on the roads" (1999, p. 10). These (and more) can and should be contested by students if complex geographical and environmental issues are to be explored, re-explored and critically questioned. And the route to such critical questioning has to be via a pedagogy that creates a culture of argument and enables students to be participants in discussion, in debate, and in the critical evaluation of alternative points of view. As Nicholson states: 'In the practice of drama, dialogic interaction allows students to "unfix", interrogate and interpret cultural meanings rather then becoming inert and passive consumers of second hand knowledge' (2000, p. 9). In order for this to happen, and for learning to be more than just short-term and superficial, students need to employ a range of social skills such as listening, articulating, co-operating, supporting and encouraging, and higher order thinking skills such as analysis, synthesis and evaluation.

For students to want to participate and to avoid the trap of passive learning they have to feel that they have something to contribute. The notion of there being different forms of intelligence (Gardner, 1993) is now widely accepted and drama lessons can engage most of them simultaneously. Stimulus resources (e.g. maps, photographs, television programmes) and discussion underpin the planning and presentation of drama activities and the development of both verbal and visual intelligence. The practical and physical nature of drama encourages those who are kinesthetically intelligent, and intrapersonal and interpersonal intelligence – the ability to understand ones own feelings and relate to the feelings of others – is often the key to the success of any drama. What we cannot do is pretend that the pedagogical processes of drama can develop all intelligences. It is possible, but less likely that mathematical intelligence will be developed through drama, and musical intelligence may only be catered for in a limited way.

Students' perceptions

Research undertaken with year 9 students on the range of learning strategies they thought made up their geographical learning at key stage 3 showed very clearly that drama, usually in the form of role play, was seldom used as a strategy for learning in the geography classroom (Adey and Biddulph, 2001). Of the 1400 students surveyed, 29% said that they rarely used role play and 62% said that they had no recollection of using role play at all. While we would expect such strategies to form only part of the teaching and learning repertoire, these figures are in stark contrast to those for non-drama strategies which students could recall using in geography lessons. Sixty-nine per cent of respondents cited copying, for example, as almost always or frequently a feature of their geography lessons. Working from textbooks was cited by 74.3 %, using worksheets by 69.2% and using teacher-produced booklets by 35%. Overall, students' perceptions of learning in geography is that it consists of a lot of writing, only some of which is creative/empathetic, that there are quite a lot of 'question and answer' sessions (59%), and a lot of teacher-led explanations (79%).

Examples of the students' comments are as follows:

- 'I didn't like working out of textbooks all of the time.'
- 'Working through endless booklets and sheets which basically said the same thing.'
- 'Looking in books and writing loads of stuff for nothing.'
- 'I didn't enjoy long drawn-out projects where you were told what you had to do and just write it down. I also disliked copying out of books.'

The overall message from students is that they perceive their key stage 3 experiences to be largely passive. However, they liked being given access to a variety of activities that enabled them to be participants in their own learning. They liked discussing their ideas with each other and the teacher, researching their own information, and 'being involved'.

- 'I really enjoyed talking to Rachel from Monserrat as it was more interesting and asking questions to a real person who has experience of a topic than working from a work or fact book.'

- 'I most enjoyed finding out about different countries and then presenting the information either doing role plays or news reports.'
- 'I enjoyed doing the live news report. We were recording it live on a video recorder.'
- 'Doing a weather lesson when we had to go up the front and explain what was happening.'

Nicholson (2000) refers to 'the culture of participation' where the pedagogy of drama enables students to work collaboratively with each other and the teacher in an active way. What the quotes from students describe is their enjoyment of learning, which is experiential (Kolb, 1984) and participative: through the process of the drama *experience* students become *participants* in their own learning.

Subsequent interviews with groups of year 8 students revealed that most (although not all) of them felt that drama often provided the opportunity to talk with their peers about the work in hand, which in turn enhanced their understanding. The process of preparing for and participating in drama where they considered a geographical issue or event required them to work in small groups. Students were clear that they enjoyed learning in such ways as it was more fun - a change from more usual types of activity they associated with geography – and that it developed skills and understandings in a unique way.

- 'It lets us get into character. We can argue and we can work together.'
- 'You can understand things in more detail - like the rainforest debate we had.'
- 'It's creative and you can bring your own ideas to it rather than just reading from a textbook.'.

So, while enjoyment was key to students' appreciation of drama-type lessons, the question is did they actually learn anything? The next chapter discusses assessment of learning.

Photo: Peter Fox (Please note the quality of this image is low because it is taken from digital video source)

6: Ideas for assessment

Formative assessment

Formative assessment has been the subject of much discussion recently. In their summary of the literature, Black and William (1998a) argue that formative assessment can be the means by which standards can be raised. For assessment to be formative it needs to:

- generate information that can improve teaching;
- produce information to help students understand their own learning potential;
- be the basis for both effective feedback on learning and feed-forward on how to improve; and
- provide opportunities for students to be involved in their own assessment and to monitor their own achievements.

(Adapted from: Lambert and Lines, 2000.)

Drama activities in geography encourage teachers to use a wide range of assessment strategies and to use assessment formatively. They open up opportunities for students to demonstrate their geographical understanding in a range of ways and thus provide teachers with different forms of evidence of geographical understanding.

Classroom assessment as part of formative assessment

Classroom assessment is an continuous part of teachers' work and it can be the means by which a great deal of learning takes place. Within drama lessons teachers have many opportunities to check out, clarify and challenge students' different levels of geographical understanding.

Let us take the sequence of lessons on coastal management as an example (see pages 30-31). The setting-up phase, where students begin to consider the different views of interested parties, provides the teacher with the time and structure which enables them to sit with small groups and listen to ideas, challenge any assumptions and move thinking on. The opportunity for direct feedback to support learning is there.

The planning phase also provides time for discussions between students and between the students and the teacher. Despite the apparently informal nature of such interactions they generate essential information on matters such as students' misconceptions, confusion surrounding a particular point of view, or the very sophisticated levels of understanding of some students. This information can in turn inform the how and the why of any subsequent interventions by the teacher to ensure that individual needs are met.

The constant process of discussion-modification-reformulation, which is characteristic of these phases, allows for what Black and Wiliam describe as 'teaching through interaction' (1998b, p. 8). When such interactions are 'thoughtful, reflective, focused to evoke and explore understanding and conducted so that all students have the opportunity to think and to express their ideas' (Black and Wiliam, 1998b, p. 7) then assessment becomes a more formative process.

Creative writing

Creative writing is a common form of assessment of many of the ideas discussed in this book. It usually starts with reflection and debriefing, giving the class a chance to join their interpretations and imaginations together as they come to grips with some of the complex ideas encountered in the drama. Leat (1998) and Leat and Kinninment (2000) emphasise the importance of debriefing as the means by which students become conscious of their own thinking – it enables them to begin to operate at a metacognitive level. High quality de-briefing is characterised by the use of a large number of open-ended questions and students having the opportunity to give extended responses. The use of open-ended questions such as 'Why do these individuals support this solution to coastal erosion?' or 'What are the longer term consequences for opting for a particular solution? How do you know this?' or 'In what ways will certain solutions impact on different interest groups?' require students to look beyond the simple and begin to consider the nuances of the issues under study. The feeling is that without some form of de-briefing process, opportunities to tease out the detail and to reflect on the outcomes are lost.

Following de-briefing, the writing tasks can be open-ended and allow students of all abilities to demonstrate their learning. As for any piece of writing, clear assessment criteria are essential from the outset and some students can also be given a writing frame to help them structure their ideas. Writing tasks can take the form of a report for the local paper, an e-mail to a website, a diary kept over the critical period of the action, a weather forecast reporting the reality and stories around a drought/heat wave, a storyline for a five-minute documentary, discussion points for a round-table meeting, 'A day in the life of ...'. The opportunities are endless.

Feedback from the student teachers showed that, in follow-up written tasks students were able to do the following: synthesise and empathise with other people's points of view, understand that there are no simple solutions to complex issues, and write imaginatively using their geographical knowledge appropriately.

Figure 5: Student's work from the coastal management lesson.

Save our Beaches!

At a meeting of the Norfolk Coastal Management group last night members of the public and other groups came together to talk about how to manage our eroding coastline. The meeting took place in Overstrand where a road had ended up falling on to a beach and houses were in danger. The erosion of the coast was caused by the type of rock which was soft in places, and the sea, and this could continue.

Several group were there including a local builder, a local hotel manager, Professor Smith – a coast expert, a coastal engineer and a group of local residents who are affected by the erosion.

Different groups had different ideas about what to do. Some of the choices included building rock groynes and rock armour – using very hard rock to protect the coast, timber revetments, beach nourishment – to replace lost sand, gabions – baskets of rock that let water drain through them, or cliff drains.

Professor Smith thought that groynes were effective but could not be used everywhere.

The tourists were in favour of beach nourishment because they felt this would give them more beach to enjoy, but the coastal engineer said that this it wouldn't work. The tourists were quite angry about this.

At one point in the meeting a hotel manager said that we had to be careful because we needed the tourists. But Professor Smith said we had to do what was best for the coast as this would also be good for the visitors. Local residents agreed with this as the erosion of the coast affects the roads they drive on and even some homes. They were also worried as their houses were not worth as much as before.

Both Professor Smith and the coastal engineer said that the best way to protect the coast here was to drain some of the clay so it would dry out a bit and then build a rock armour revetment where the tough rock could arrive to the beach by sea. This would make a very strong form of protection.

It was eventually agreed to take the advice of the experts even though a nicer beach would have been fun to have.

The example of work shown in Figure 5 demonstrates the students' ability to use quite technical vocabulary appropriately and their understanding that different potential solutions to the problem exist. They seem to recognise the difference between 'the expert' as opposed to 'interest group', and they also establish that some opinions are more important than others. Their empathy with local residents and their appreciation of the conflict between different groups is in evidence. This example indicates that the students' have identified that, at times, some groups will hold similar opinions and that this collaboration can be influential in the decision making process.

Assessing practical work

The drama process itself – the presentational element - can also provide opportunities for assessment and reflection. The use of a video camera can add a sense of reality to any performance (in fact several of the student teachers interviewed said that they wished they had used a camera) and can also be a vehicle to capture the geographical learning for later review and evaluation. Processes such as freeze-framing, and thought-tracking and questioning of an 'expert', can all provide the teacher with continuing evidence of students' understanding and enable them to use this evidence to adjust their teaching. The use of a digital camera can make available to students images of their own and other people's performance, which in turn can support debriefing discussions and any subsequent written work. Images taken during the land-use conflict lesson served to support the de-briefing that took place during the subsequent lesson – they were a reference point for students' ideas and served to support follow-up work. Image annotation, discussion of images and written work built around the events within the image can all serve to highlight geographical understanding and can add a greater sense of purpose to the drama activity.

The performance aspect of drama-geography lessons can be a vehicle for many to shine, especially those who struggle with writing tasks. And so assessment of geographical learning should not rely solely on written outcomes. How to assess drama and give formative feedback to students is no easy task, but the use of rubrics can be a useful way forward.

Rubrics are descriptions of criteria for different levels of performance. According to Star (2003), some of the qualities of a good rubric would be that it:

- addresses all relevant content and performance objectives;
- defines standards and helps students to achieve them via explicit criteria;
- is easy to understand and use;
- provides all with the opportunity to succeed at some level;
- enables students to evaluate their own performance.

Figure 6 provides a rubric that could be used with the lesson on coastal management (see pages 30-31).

While the content of this rubric may look like yet more level descriptions, the absence of a grading system (although one can be added if this is felt necessary) enables the rubric to be used for a different purpose. Such a table can be shared with students at the start of the sequence of lessons so that they know what they are working towards. It can be a constant reference point during subsequent lessons, and during the drama presentations the teacher can simply circle relevant boxes and give almost immediate feedback to groups on their practical work. Alternatively, students could assess their own practical work by circling those statements that they feel best reflect their performance.

Such a rubric is specific to an individual or a sequence of lessons. However, criteria can be added, taking into account the preparation phase as well as the performance, or a box for student reflection could also be added.

Criteria	Description			
Use of geographical terminology	Accurate and confident use of a range of relevant terminology including: groynes, gabions, revetments, seawalls, beach nourishment, boreholes, cliff drains. Examples used to demonstrate understanding	Accurate use of a range of relevant terminology including: groynes, gabions, revetments, seawalls, beach nourishment, boreholes, cliff drains	Use of some of the following relevant terminology: groynes, breakwaters, seawalls, gabions, revetments, boreholes, cliff drains	Some key terminology is tentatively used, but not always in the right context
Understanding of the different points of view relating to different methods of coastal management	Communicates ideas from all of the major interest groups, adding detail from independent research	Communicates ideas from all of the major interest groups	Communicates ideas from all of the major interest groups	Most points of view are communicated, some lack detail
Articulation of the arguments for and against different methods of coastal management	Range of ideas and how they conflict and agree is communicated. Detailed reference to examples from the case study to support arguments	Range of ideas and how they conflict and agree is communicated. Some reference to examples to support arguments	Range of ideas and how they conflict and agree is communicated. Examples not always well used	The arguments are presented in a limited way Examples from the case study are not used
Use of appropriate materials such as maps, photographs and diagrams to support the presentation	Reference made to accurate, relevant and well-presented support materials	Reference made to accurate, relevant and well-presented support materials	Reference made to relevant support materials. A lot of dependence on non-geographical props to support the presentation	Some support materials are evident but not used to support the presentation
Creative presentation adopting a particular genre to communicate ideas and understanding	Genre within which the group are working is clear to the audience. Characters are convincingly portrayed	Genre within which the group are working is clear to the audience. Characters are convincingly portrayed	Genre within which the group are working is clear to the audience. Characters not really convincingly portrayed	Genre is not clear and characterisation is unrealistic and unconvincing

Figure 6:
A rubric to assess student understanding of coastal management via drama.

What this rubric does is make clear the geographical criteria on which students will be assessed, as well as the drama. As such it can help students to avoid over-emphasis on the 'drama' at the expense of the geography.

A rubric like the one shown in Figure 6 can assist teachers and students in judging levels of geographical understanding in drama activities. What is also needed is a clear indication of how students can improve. The criteria themselves signify what needs to be done in order to achieve an improvement; however, it is only when such a table is used to support dialogue between student and teacher that assessment is truly formative.

Photo: Peter Fox (Please note the quality of this image is low because it is taken from digital video source)

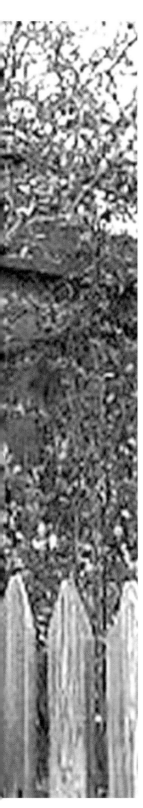

7: Conclusion

Using drama strategies to help students both to enjoy geography lessons and to develop their geographical understanding is not easy. It can be time consuming and it requires a great deal of commitment and energy on the part of teachers and students. It is also fair to say that not all students enjoy drama. It can be too public and fear of 'making a fool of myself' is very real for some young people.

In terms of learning geography, the evidence from the student teachers who took part in the activities described here was that drama activities provided key stage 3 students with the opportunity to demonstrate their geographical understanding in a unique way. They all felt that the school students used and applied new geographical vocabulary appropriately, understood the nature and the nuances of conflict and asked some incisive geographical questions. They also engaged in thoughtful and thought-provoking discussion. The social benefits were evident because some students displayed confidence and abilities never seen before and the motivation to participate was, in the main, high.

Drama strategies can provide opportunities for the structured use of creative talk in the classroom where students are encouraged to use their imagination, employ their social skills and challenge their cognitive ability through the shared and creative exploration of geographical concepts. While tapping into the geographies of the environment, of other people and other places and other events, drama strategies also contribute to students' understanding of geographical enquiry (Roberts, 2003) and Citizenship (Biddulph, 2001). What is most important perhaps is that drama gives students a voice: to express their feelings, to contest geographical givens, to articulate their concerns and to be inspired. In being given their own voice young people can begin to feel empowered to understand the voices of others.

Bibliography

Adey, K. and Biddulph, M. (2001) 'The influence of student perceptions on subject choice at 14+ in geography and history', *Educational Studies*, 27, 4, pp. 439-50.

Balderstone, D. (2000) 'Teaching styles and strategies' in Kent, A. (ed) *Reflective Practice in Geography Teaching*. London: Paul Chapman, pp. 113-30.

Biddulph, M. and Clark, J. (forthcoming) 'Drama in the geography classroom' in Balderstone, D. (ed) *Teaching and Learning in Geography*. Sheffield: Geographical Association.

Biddulph, M. (2001) 'Citizenship education: pedagogical questions' in Lambert, D. and Machon, P. (eds) *Citizenship through Secondary Geography*. London: RoutledgeFalmer, pp. 182-96.

Black, P. and Wiliam, D. (1998a) 'Inside the black box: raising standards through classroom assessment' (available online at http://www.pdkintl.org/kappan/kbla9810.htm).

Black, P. and Wiliam, D. (1998b) 'Assessment and classroom learning', *Assessment in Education, 5*, 1, pp. 7-74.

Butt, G. (2001) *Theory into Practice: Extending writing skills*. Sheffield: Geographical Association.

Coyle, D. (1996) 'Language medium teaching in Britain' in Fruhauf, G., Coyle, D. and Christ, I. (eds) *Teaching Content in a Foreign Language – Practice and perspectives in European bilingual education*. Onderwijs: Stiching Europees Platform voor het Nederlandse.

Department for Education and Employment/Qualifications and Curriculum Authority (DfEE/QCA) (1999a) *Geography: The National Curriculum for England (key stages 1-3)*. London: HMSO.

DfEE/Standards and Effectiveness Unit (SEU) (2001) *Literacy Across the Curriculum: Training materials*. London: DfEE/SEU.

Durbin, C. (2003) 'Creativity - criticism and challenge in geography', *Teaching Geography*, 28, 2, pp. 64-9.

Gardner, H. (1993) *Multiple Intelligences. The theory in practice*. New York: Basic Books.

Joyce, B., Weil, M. and Calhoun, E. (2000) *Models of Teaching* (sixth edition). Boston: Allyn and Bacon.

Joyce, B., Calhoun, E. and Hopkins, D. (2002) *Models of Learning, Tools for Teaching* (second edition). Buckingham: Open University Press.

Kolb, D. (1984) *Experiential Learning*. London: Prentice Hall.

Lambert, D. (1999) 'Geography and moral education in a supercomplex world: the significance of values education and some remaining dilemmas', *Ethics, Place and Environment*, 2, 1, pp. 5-18.

Lambert, D. and Lines, D. (2000) *Understanding Assessment: Purpose, perceptions, practice*. London: RoutledgeFalmer.

Leat, D. (1998) *Thinking Through Geography*. Cambridge: Chris Kington Publishing.

Leat, D. and Kinninment, D. (2000) 'Learn to debrief' in Fisher, C. and Binns, T. (eds) *Issues in Teaching Geography*. London: RoutledgeFalmer, pp. 152-72.

NATE Drama Committee (2000) *Cracking Drama: Progression in drama within English*. Sheffield: National Association for the Teaching of English.

Neelands, J. (1992) *Learning Through Imagined Experience: The role of drama in the national curriculum*. London: Hodder and Stoughton.

Nicholson, H. (2000) *Teaching Drama 11-18*. London: Continuum.

Rawling, E. and Westaway, J. (2003) 'Exploring creativity', *Teaching Geography*, 28, 1, pp. 5-8.

Roberts, M. (1986) 'Talking, reading and writing' in Boardman, D. (ed) *Handbook for Geography Teachers*. Sheffield: Geographical Association, pp. 68-78.

Roberts, M. (1996) 'Teaching styles and strategies' in Kent, A., Lambert, D., Naish, M. and Slater, F. (eds) *Geography in Education: Viewpoints on teaching and learning*. Cambridge: Cambridge University Press, pp. 231-59.

Roberts, M. (2003) *Learning through Enquiry: Making sense of geography in the key stage 3 classroom*. Sheffield: Geographical Association.

QCA/DfES (2000) Schemes of Work at www.standards.dfes.gov.uk/schemes3/

Shulman, L. (1999) 'Knowledge and teaching: foundations of the new reform' in Leach, J. and Moon, B. (eds) *Learners and Pedadagogy*. London. Open University.

Starr, L. (2003) 'Creating rubrics: tools you can use' (available online at http://www.education-world.com/a_curr/curr248.shtml).

Taylor, K. (1991) *Drama Strategies*. Oxford: Heinemann Educational.

Vygotsky, L. (1962) *Thought and Language*. Cambridge MA: the Massachusetts Institute of Technology Press.